# THE REAL PRESENCE

*OR*

## THE LOCALISATION IN CULTUS
## OF THE DIVINE PRESENCE

T0382326

*O Lord, pardon my three sins.*
*I have in contemplation clothed in form Thee who art formless:*
*I have in praise described Thee who art ineffable:*
*And in visiting shrines I have ignored Thine omnipresence.*

(Sankara, eighth cent. A.D. India.)

# THE REAL PRESENCE

*OR*

## THE LOCALISATION IN CULTUS
## OF THE DIVINE PRESENCE

by

## A. C. BOUQUET, D.D.

*Trinity College, Cambridge*
*Hulsean Lecturer*
*1924–5*

CAMBRIDGE

AT THE UNIVERSITY PRESS

1928

## CAMBRIDGE
### UNIVERSITY PRESS

University Printing House, Cambridge CB2 8BS, United Kingdom

Published in the United States of America by Cambridge University Press, New York

Cambridge University Press is part of the University of Cambridge.

It furthers the University's mission by disseminating knowledge in the pursuit of
education, learning and research at the highest international levels of excellence.

www.cambridge.org
Information on this title: www.cambridge.org/9781107426801

© Cambridge University Press 1928

This publication is in copyright. Subject to statutory exception
and to the provisions of relevant collective licensing agreements,
no reproduction of any part may take place without the written
permission of Cambridge University Press.

First published 1928
First paperback edition 2014

*A catalogue record for this publication is available from the British Library*

ISBN 978-1-107-42680-1 Paperback

Cambridge University Press has no responsibility for the persistence or accuracy of
URLs for external or third-party internet websites referred to in this publication,
and does not guarantee that any content on such websites is, or will remain, accurate
or appropriate.

CONTENTS

# NOTE

A PORTION *of this book was read in the first instance as a paper to the Cambridge University Theological Society. In response to a number of requests for its publication I now present it in a revised and slightly enlarged form, with the addition of some further extracts in illustration of the subject, and also a few notes based on the discussion which followed the reading of the paper. My main object is to lay before the educated Christian public the facts about localisation, and to enable them to decide for themselves without prejudice the proper place which sacramental ordinances should occupy in the religious life.*

*I desire to acknowledge the courtesy of Messrs Jonathan Cape, Mr Humphrey Milford, Messrs Methuen and Co., and the Hakluyt Society in allowing me to make quotations from works published by them; I have also to thank the Westminster Trustees for leave to include the extract from* The Light Invisible; *and finally I am indebted to the Rev. J. S. Boys-Smith for kindly reading the proofs and making suggestions.*

A. C. BOUQUET

CAMBRIDGE

MAY    1928

# THE REAL PRESENCE

===

## INTRODUCTION

The subject of this essay is the theory and implications of localisation in cultus.

(1) I would begin it with a plea that in philosophising upon religion we should not neglect the raw material which lies about us. It is not enough to shut our eyes with Descartes and examine our internal sensations and theorise about what ought to be outside. We must not exclude from our survey the habits and experiences of other religious persons than ourselves, nor must we restrict our attention to the New Testament, though that in itself should be better esteemed by the philosopher than it has hitherto been.

(2) In the second place it will be fairly obvious that my subject has been supplied by more or less recent controversy. I do not suggest that such controversy is the main

cause of this essay, since the possibility of an enquiry of the kind which I now propose has occurred to me for a considerable time, and the stir of the last few months has only quickened my sense of the need for a discussion of the problems relating to worship in theory and practice which shall be conducted in an academic spirit and with an absence of bitterness and heat. On the one hand we hear of people being pained and shocked because their devotional practices are compared to those of educated Hindus, when it seems extremely probable that they do not know how educated Hindus behave. On the other hand we read denunciations of idolatry which leave the impression that those who utter them have not really thought out what idolatry means: there has been little or no attempt to undertake a serious study of the problem in a mood of philosophic calm.

I propose then for our discussion the nature and implications of the cultus of the deity by means of the direction of attention upon concrete objects, or in other words the localisation of worship. The word "idolatry" does not altogether express what I have in mind. Localisation will serve better as a label. We may also consider the causes of reaction against such localisation. Can they be traced to a common root? Is iconoclasm more creditable than iconolatry, or is the one as good as the other? Can we detect any laws governing the swing of the pendulum in either direction? Assuming that the cultus of a localised presence is agreed to have no specially divine sanction, and that the mechanism by which it satisfies the instincts of the worshipper is understood, should it be tolerated? What is the significance of the stern denunciation of images which characterises the utterances of the Hebrew prophets and their spiritual kinsmen? Are we to posit two equally permissible types of worshippers, who will nevertheless always tend to disagree? These are questions which my own Anglican (as much as my Huguenot) forefathers would hardly have allowed. They

[ 3 ]    1-2

took it for granted that the matter had been settled in one way at the Reformation. We to-day of whatever denomination can hardly afford to dismiss the matter so lightly. We have a wider range of facts before our eyes. We need to ask these questions, and to frame our own answers to them. Even if in the end we arrive at the same position as the reformers we shall probably do so by a different path and for different reasons.

The problem which we are to consider is a special case of a more general problem which reappears in at least four other forms.

(*a*) The unique local incarnation of the deity in one special human being.

(*b*) The periodicity of the religious consciousness involving as it would seem seasons of temporary inspiration.

(*c*) The restriction of revelation to, or at least its intensification in, the recorded words of a sacred writing, book, or group of books, often the less understood the better.

(*d*) The conception of finality in religion as manifested at a particular point in history.

# INTRODUCTION

A large part of our time will be taken up with the hearing of what various witnesses have to say on the subject.

## THE ATTITUDE WHICH WE HAVE INHERITED

Let us consider first the attitude which we have inherited. The reformed churches uniformly adopted the attitude of the Jews towards images, pictures, or localised sacramental worship. In general they may be said to have modelled their behaviour on the injunctions which are to be found in the Acts of the Apostles (Acts xiv. 15 ; xvii. 29 ; xix. 26), i.e. "to turn from these vain things to the living God." This corresponds well with the Anglican appeal to the primitive church, though it does not fit in with an appeal to the church of the first six centuries or even of the first four. It is natural to compare the official Anglican homily ("against peril of idolatry"), a very elaborate historical survey based on the treatise by Bullinger on the same subject. The universal assumption in reformed circles is that localisation in cultus (except apparently in church buildings)[1] is wrong under all circumstances and is expressly forbidden by Almighty God.

On the other hand by far the largest organised bodies of Christians have for centuries practised a form of localised worship, and have a defence of it to offer. We may briefly recall that the period 725–847 in the Eastern Church, during which the iconoclastic controversy raged, ended in an alliance between the Pope and the Byzantine Christians, the Pope advocating in unmistakable terms the use of images for instruction of the ignorant and encouragement of the faithful. The distinction however was drawn by the orthodox theologians between the worship due to God alone which is called "λατρεία" and that which is due to holy objects such as images of Christ and the

---

[1] Even here the passage quoted from 1 Kings would doubtless have been quoted as signifying that what happened in a church or chapel was not a localising of God's Presence, but of human attention to His Universal Presence.

Saints, the book of the Gospels, the Cross
and Crucifix and holy pictures or Icons. To
these was to be accorded "$\sigma\chi\epsilon\tau\iota\kappa\dot{\eta}$" or
"$\tau\iota\mu\eta\tau\iota\kappa\dot{\eta}\ \pi\rho\sigma\sigma\kappa\acute{\upsilon}\nu\eta\sigma\iota\varsigma$," or, as perhaps we
should say in English, reverence rather than
worship. At a later date a further distinction
was drawn between the reverence due to
be paid to the humanity of Christ Himself
which was described as "$\acute{\upsilon}\pi\epsilon\rho\delta\sigma\upsilon\lambda\epsilon\acute{\iota}\alpha$" and
that which might be offered to the Saints
which was described as "$\delta\sigma\upsilon\lambda\epsilon\acute{\iota}\alpha$." Later still
in the thirteenth century it was further de-
termined that Christ was to be worshipped
with $\lambda\alpha\tau\rho\epsilon\acute{\iota}\alpha$ (a word which in good classi-
cal Greek is used to express the service due
to the gods); while $\acute{\upsilon}\pi\epsilon\rho\delta\sigma\upsilon\lambda\epsilon\acute{\iota}\alpha$ might be
paid to Blessed Mary the Mother of Christ.
These distinctions obviously qualify the
nature of the $\pi\rho\sigma\sigma\kappa\acute{\upsilon}\nu\eta\sigma\iota\varsigma$ paid to symbols
of the various persons respectively referred
to. It is to be noted at this point that $\pi\rho\sigma\sigma$-
$\kappa\acute{\upsilon}\nu\eta\sigma\iota\varsigma$ is not an unknown word in the
Gospels, but is applied to the young man
who came and kneeled before Jesus. It is

not really in origin a religious term but means the act of making a profound obeisance before one's superior. Josephus speaks of the Jewish High Priests as προσκυνούμενοι. Προσκύνησις was given to the Byzantine emperor, who was solemnly censed and received prostrations and kissing of the feet. On the other hand in 1 Cor. xiv. 25 and Revelation xi. 16 we get the verb used with reference to τῷ θεῷ; so that the usage is not precise or consistent. The Roman Catholic Catechism says that we should give to relics, crucifixes and holy pictures a relative honour as they relate to Christ and His Saints and are memorials of them, but it adds: "we do not pray to relics or images for they can neither see nor hear nor help us." It further declares that the first commandment does not forbid the making of images but the making of idols; that is, making images to be adored or honoured as gods. The theory therefore would seem to be that προσκύνησις is the technical equivalent of relative honour, but that λατρεία is not to be accorded to any localised object except the divine presence in the Eucharistic symbols, which, according to the view summarised in the decrees of Trent, is in an entirely different category. The Anglican Church, as Jeremy Taylor has clearly pointed out[1], has not officially accepted this theory, but has until recently followed the rigorous line of the Puritans, both as regards images and as regards the sacramental elements.

### ICONOCLASM

The opposition to localisation in cultus which we sometimes call iconoclasm derives to all appearance solely from the prophetic element in Judaism[2]. There is no sure evidence of any independent source. Some have even thought that the reforming Egyptian king Ikhnaton may have come under the influence of Hebrew ideas, and that Islam in India may have influenced Sankara. It is

[1] In *Ductor Dubitantium*.

[2] The pagan philosopher of late antiquity might scorn image-worship for himself, but like the modern Hindu philosopher he would allow it to the proletariat.

therefore desirable to consider a little the reaction of Hebrew religion against localisation. Popular pre-exilic religion localised the divine presence freely, and the distinction between the popular and the higher prophetic view shows that the latter was far from being universally accepted. The Semitic temperament is not universally iconoclastic, as may be seen from the pages of Robertson Smith. Irrespective of the bull images and other emblems there was the cloud which was believed to rest on the mercy seat above the ark. Whatever the nature of this phenomenon there can be no doubt that some localised presence was connected with it. Nevertheless the prophets are steadfastly opposed to the conceptions underlying these practices and seldom lose an opportunity of testifying to their inadequacy. It may fairly be said, however, that in the documents which have come down to us the Hebrew race is represented as recognising varying types and degrees of intensity in its experience of the divine pre-

sence. We have on the one hand the type
represented in the 139th Psalm, "Whither
shall I go then from thy spirit...thy presence," and the saying on the other hand,
"The Lord is in His holy temple, the Lord's
seat is in heaven."

The logical outcome of the higher prophetic teaching is the development of the
doctrine that God in the essence of His being
is aloof from the world, and that it is an in-
dignity to Him to suppose that He can have
direct contact with inert matter, and im-
mediate intercourse with sinful man, and so
gradually He is pushed further away from
His world: or perhaps we may more justly
say that the Divine Being so overshadows and
dwarfs everything in His creation that He
may very properly be described as having His
centre everywhere and His circumference
nowhere and thus be too great for definition.
Such beliefs in India led to the feeling that
God was not really known, nor could He
be known, and they were thus compatible
with the toleration of a large amount of

localised and idolatrous worship on the part of the masses. This, however, ceased to be the case among the Jews especially in the two centuries immediately preceding the death of Christ. The extreme doctrine of transcendence reaches its maximum in the writings of Philo, who maintains that to assign any quality to God is to limit Him. The result of this may be seen in the Targums where the writer shrinks from any suggestion that God can be localised even in heaven. The text in I Kings viii. 27, "The heaven of heavens cannot contain Thee," is freely accepted as the authority for this. Similarly God cannot be said to remove or withdraw from any place. In order therefore to account for the experiences of human beings in which they seemed to be aware of the divine presence in connection with a material object or a defined space or locality, the Jew as is well known developed the conception of the Shekinah (that which dwells or resides), and there is little doubt that the Greek word "σκηνή" was used by bi-lingual

Jews as a translation of it. The corresponding verb is used in John i. 14 of the incarnation and again in Revelation xxi. 3. There seems also strong probability that the word "δόξα" is also used to represent the idea of the Shekinah (see especially Hebrews i. 3, Romans vi. 4, and James ii. 1). It is as though the philosophic Jew, being unable to limit the divine presence in theory, found it necessary in practice to assume that at certain times and places there was a concentration or knotting or discontinuity, in which the glory of God was specially perceivable. In Philo this theory takes the form of the Logos-doctrine which as is well known gradually develops onwards from him (with Gentile affinities), the Logos being a kind of concentrated yet totally divine intermediary between the finite creature and the absolute and indefinable deity. This it will be seen harmonises well with the view of Professor Rudolf Otto to which I will presently refer, but it is plain that there is a distinction between the perception of God in some locality of His own choice, and the selection by the worshipper of some tangible object without of necessity the previous sanction of the deity having been obtained, though this latter practice may mean that the individual, by attending to the omnipresent Reality in relation to a particular time or spot or circumstance, may in this way seem but *only* seem to limit and localise that Reality.

Dean Inge in his essay on St Paul remarks that idolatry is an aid to worship which is quite innocent and natural in some peoples but which the Jews never understood. The typical phrase by which the Jew describes his conception of God as contrasted with that of the idolaters is "the living God" (אֵל חָי). Sometimes the phrase is in the plural (אֱלֹהִים חַיִּים), whatever that may signify—perhaps royalty—as in Deuteronomy v. 26 and 2 Kings xix. 4 and 16, but there are a number of instances of the singular both in the Hebrew and in the Greek. In the Septuagint it occurs eight times, and in

the New Testament we find more or less
exact parallels in Acts xiv. 15, and also
Hebrews ix. 14, in addition to which we
get the three important phrases, Matthew
xvi. 16 (ὁ υἱὸς τοῦ θεοῦ τοῦ ζῶντος), John vi.
57 (ὁ ζῶν πατήρ), and Revelation i. 18
(ἐγὼ εἰμὶ...ὁ ζῶν).

It seems probable that the original phrase
bears some relation to the divine tetragram-
maton of Exodus iii, but in effect the main
contrast indicated is between The Invisible
Living Spirit who is continually unfolding
Himself and even seems to experience development, and the dead image of wood or
stone. It is possible to maintain that the
Jews were to some extent unfair in their
estimate of the use made of images. The use
of a visible object for purposes of concentration may be quite harmless if that object is
employed, as it often is, simply as a means to
an end, for in such a case the worshipper passes
beyond it, making it so to speak a bridge
by which to get across into touch with the
omnipresent Reality. On the other hand

there is undoubtedly the danger of stopping short and allowing the visible image to limit one's idea of the nature of God, and the religious type which prefers using no visible symbol is undoubtedly irritated by the sight of other people of an entirely different temperament carrying an image in procession and paying it ceremonial honours.

We see then that the steadfast rejection of acts of reverence to any local objects derives entirely from the prophetic tradition among the Jewish Semites. There is no reason for supposing that Mohammed obtained his intense feeling of opposition to idolatry from any other source than a certain Semitic desire for imageless worship. It is generally agreed that it was at any rate indirectly the influence of Islam which produced the iconoclastic movement of the eighth century. The Emperor Leo III had been brought into intimate association with the Saracens, and to some enthusiasts Moslem worship actually seemed at the time to be more spiritual than Christian worship. It

is obvious that it was almost entirely
the revival of the study of the Scriptures
which determined the attitude of the Protestant world towards the reverence of local
symbols. The iconoclastic fanaticism of the
Sikhs in India derives from Islam and so
from Judaism, and is an attempt to reform
Hinduism in a Moslem direction. The Protestant view of localised symbols has found
a ready acceptance on the part of many
pagan races throughout the world, and
while there can be no denying the capacity
of Catholic and Orthodox missionaries to
make converts and construct native churches
on the basis of προσκύνησις we are equally
bound to recognise the enormous vitality
and expansion of the Protestant churches.
It is hardly an over-statement to say that
without the iconoclastic motive a large part
of the enthusiasm with which these churches
prosecute their missionary work would be
cut away. The influence of prophetic Judaism is therefore of almost incalculable
magnitude, and it is this influence which,

as we shall see, conflicts seriously with the
practices of natural religion. Indeed the
question may well be asked whether any
synthesis is possible which will enable a
fair-minded student of religion to include
both methods of approach without doing
injustice to either. The distinction is often
quite properly made between worship which
stops short at the symbol and worship
which proceeds through the symbol to
God. But the iconoclastic worshipper will
have none of this distinction. To him the
symbol is ever a danger and he rejects even
its limited use. We have then the remarkable
fact that iconoclasm, while deriving from
one source racially, shows a most remarkable
tendency to invade the territory occupied by
the cultus of emblems, to establish itself
there, and even to push out this cultus
with varying degrees of success. Here, it
seems, we have a psychological problem
which I venture to think cannot be solved
simply along racial lines. It is, for example,
not enough to say that the Nordic inclines

to Protestantism and the Iberian to Catholicism. The Iberian Cornish make good Methodists and the black Welsh too, and there are plenty of Nordic Catholics in Germany. Moreover, in Africa we have the state of Uganda divided in its allegiance between a large Roman community, a large church of Puritan Anglicans, and a considerable number of Moslems, while these denominations in no way correspond with race divisions. In East Africa the same racial type is being converted in one diocese to Protestant Anglicanism, and in another to Anglo-Catholicism. In India the same Tamil-speaking peoples can be induced to react alike to Protestant and to Catholic Christianity[1].

---

[1] I confess however to a certain degree of puzzlement at the contradictory nature of the evidence. We are told for instance (Kendrick, *Druidism*) that the Germanic element in N.E. Britain dispensed with priests and sacrifices and perhaps with idols. But how much do we really know about this? Is perhaps the absence of a priesthood simply absence of a *differentiated* priesthood? Does the alleged absence of sacrifice rest on assured evidence, and does it mean that there was no localisation in cultus?

## MODES OF CONCEIVING THE
## DIVINE PRESENCE

Let us now approach the conception of the Divine Presence by a different route and hear some evidence of a different type. We will begin with a passage from Professor Otto[1]:

We say, then, that this doctrine of the omnipresence of God—as though by a necessity of His being He must be bound to every place, like a natural force pervading space—is a frigid invention of metaphysical speculation entirely without religious import. Scripture knows nothing of it. Scripture knows no "Omnipresence," neither the expression nor the meaning it expresses; it knows only the God who is where He wills to be, and is not where He wills not to be, the "deus mobilis," who is no mere universally extended being, but an august mystery, that comes and goes, approaches and withdraws, has its time and hour, and may be far or near in infinite degrees, "closer than breathing" to us, miles remote from us. The hours of His "visitation" and His "return" are

[1] *Das Heilige*, Harvey's translation, p. 219.

[ 20 ]

rare and solemn occasions, different essentially
not only from the "profane" life of every day,
but also from the calm confiding mood of the
believer, whose trust is to live ever before the
face of God. They are the topmost summits in
the life of the Spirit. They are not only rare
occasions, they must needs be so for our sakes,
for no creature can bear often or for long the
full nearness of God's majesty in its beatitude
and in its awfulness. Yet there must still be
such times, for they show the bright vision and
completion of our sonship, they are a bliss in
themselves and potent for redemption. They are
the real sacrament, in comparison with which all
high official ceremonials, Masses, and rituals the
world over become the figurings of a child. And
a Divine Service would be the truest which led
up to such a mystery and the riches of grace
that ensue upon the realisation of it. And if it
be asked whether a Divine Service is able to
achieve this, let us answer that, though God
indeed comes where and when He chooses, yet
He will choose to come when we sincerely call
upon Him, and prepare ourselves truly for His
visitation.

It may be that we should not all express
ourselves in exactly the terms of this fine

passage, containing as it does some serious over-statements, but it is I believe a fact of universal experience that we do perceive the Divine Presence in a more acute degree when we are in a certain position or locality, or looking at some special object, or stimulated by some external action or actions. The terms by which we describe the relation of the posture, object, or action to the personality of God may not always be completely satisfactory, but it is better to seek a fuller explanation than to deny the connection. It is also a fact of experience that whatever may be theoretically held about the divine omnipresence, in practice there are very few who do not at least localise the Divine Presence by attending to it at some times and in some places rather than others. The Quaker outlook or that of Brother Lawrence is comparatively rare, though it should certainly be cultivated. It will be convenient then to consider a little the modes in which the Divine Presence has been conceived, classifying them rather according to human types than in terms of Jew and Gentile. The God of the primitives is almost always localised in a visible spot, whither man can draw near, compelled by need or desire. All simple prayer presupposes belief in the anthropomorphic habits of the deity addressed. But for the philosopher, the religious genius, and the prophet, things are different. The philosopher in particular renounces the idea of a local presence. Seneca says :

We must not raise the hands to heaven or whisper into the ear of a statue as though thereby to be better heard. God is near us, with us, and in us [1].

Schopenhauer presents the extreme critical position :

Whether one makes an idol of wood, stone, metal or abstract ideas it is all the same, it remains idolatry, so long as one holds before one

[1] Seneca would however have probably allowed localisation to the peasant. An educated Hindu said to me only a month ago, "I think animism is a very useful belief—for primitive peoples."

the concept of a personal [I think he means anthropomorphic] being to be addressed in sacrifice and prayer.

This is of course the familiar attitude of many modern thinkers.

In the third place, however, there is the mystical realisation of the Divine Presence which, though at one point it may approach that of the rationalist philosopher, at the other comes near to that of the primitive. Heiler[1] recognises a number of different types of mystical prayer which he labels respectively cult-mysticism, infinity-mysticism, quietism and marriage-mysticism. Cult-mysticism he regards as typically associated with some form of localisation. If I understand him aright he here displays his characteristically sympathetic touch due to his personal knowledge of Catholicism. He regards the cultus of sacramental symbols as a true mysticism of an extremely rich and complex type, and insists that the cultus of the tabernacle, so far from being

[1] *Das Gebet*, pp. 322 and ff.

a restriction of devotion making it meagre and materialistic, is in reality one of the most wonderful phenomena known to the history of religion, one of the hidden unconquerable springs of Catholic piety. He gives a vast number of quotations in support of this, and comments on the difference between the early church view of the sacramental presence ("something impersonal, a holy object full of wondrous life-giving power") and the medieval view of it ("completely personal, since in the sacrament was to be seen the Saviour God veiled under a visible form").

### THE EVIDENCE OF ANTHROPOLOGY

We now concentrate for a little upon the primitives. The making of images is a practice which has been explained on various grounds. It is said that the use of images in religion is not primitive but intermediary. The American expert, Toy[1], declares

---

[1] Introduction to the *Comparative Study of Religion.*

that it comes in at the stage of culture connected with the agricultural life. Imageless cultus characterises the highest and equally the lowest stages of religion, and is therefore no index of the elevation of a belief. It is however necessary to draw a distinction between the manufacture of anthropomorphic images, and the localisation of the Deity for purposes of cultus in some object which is not anthropomorphic. A further sub-division is necessary between localisation in natural objects, and localisation in manufactured objects. Thus in India we have the localisation of the Deity under all three forms. It is said that certain people have not practised the use of localisation. This assertion with regard to the majority however is probably due to a misunderstanding, since what is looked for is an image in the form of a man or animal, and where this is not found the rash assumption follows that there is no localisation, whereas in all probability a closer scrutiny would show localisation in a stone such as the lingam, if not in some natural object such as a tree[1].

The theory for the construction of images is that they represent the product of some pent-up emotion. The image is a fixation of an imaginative emotion for the purpose of holding that emotion fast[2]. Its purpose is that of Peter when he wished to build a hut on the Mount of Transfiguration. Preserve an emblem or reproduce a situation which once excited emotion, and the emotion may be prolonged or recalled whenever one reverts to the contemplation of the emblem or the dramatic situation. The assumption of primitive man seems to be that if an object has produced a certain emotion in him it will generally or always do so, and this power may be sometimes extended to all objects of the same class or shape. Such an assumption persists into higher cultural circles and has much to commend it.

[1] Something of this sort was probably the case in Ireland. The idols destroyed by St Patrick were almost certainly not anthropomorphic.

[2] See Jane Harrison, *Art and ancient Ritual*, p. 191— Apollo as Daphnephoros.

LOCALISATION IN FOOD

Let us come now to consider the practice of localisation in food.

The establishment as a scientific fact of the collateral and independent evolution of religious practices is undoubtedly one of the greatest results of the comparative method of studying religious phenomena. The evolution of the sacramental meal and the cultus of food in many different parts of the world along parallel lines are no longer to be regarded as a sign of dependence, but may quite rightly be considered as due to the collateral and independent workings of the human mind in different places over a wide area.

The details may be read in volumes devoted to the comparative study of religions, and, so far as I am able to discover, the facts are undisputed. I give the details from Professor Jevons[1], though many of them reappear in the pages of Sir James Frazer.

The first stage in the development of this

---

[1] Jevons, *History of Religion*, ch. xvi.

form of the sacramental meal is that in which the plant totem or vegetation spirit has not yet come to be conceived of as having human form.

In this stage the seeds or fruit are eaten at a solemn annual meal, of which all members of the community (clan or family) must eat, and of which no fragments must be left—two conditions essential, as we have seen, in the sacrificial meal of the animal totem. Of this stage we have a survival in the Lithuanian feast Samborios. Annually in December, in each household, a mess consisting of wheat, barley, oats and other seeds was cooked; of it none but members of the household could partake, and every member must partake; nothing might be left, or if left the remains must be buried. A similar survival was the Athenian Pyanepsion, an annual feast (occurring at the end of the procession in which the eiresionê was carried) in which also a mess of all sorts of cereals (Πάνσπερμα) was cooked and consumed by the household. In Sicily the Kotytis feast had degenerated considerably. Like the Athenian feast it began with a procession in which the branch of a tree was carried round the community, but the only trace of the original

meal of which all were expected to partake was
the practice of throwing the fruits, which had
been attached to the branch, to be scrambled for
by the people. In the New World Chicomecoate's
feast in April began with a procession of youths
carrying stalks of maize and other herbs through
the maize-fields; and then a mess of tortillas,
chian flour, maize and beans was eaten in the
goddess's temple in a general scramble, take who
could[1].

The second stage is that in which the
food is artificially manufactured into the
image of a human form. The stories related
by the Jesuit Father Acosta of the customs
connected with Mexican religious obser-
vances are so remarkable that I do not think
I can do better than reproduce the whole
of the two principal passages as they appear
in the Old English translation of Grimston[2].

It is a thing more worth admiration to heare
speak of the feast and solemnitie of the Com-

[1] Probably we get a degenerate survival of some such
primitive religious custom in the Shrove Tuesday
"pan-cake greaze" at Westminster School.
[2] Published by the Hakluyt Society. Chs. xxiii and
xxiv.

munion which the Divel himselfe, the Prince of
Pride, ordayned in Mexico, the which (although
it bee somewhat long) yet shall it not bee from
the purpose to relate, as it is written by men of
credite. The Mexicaines in the moneth of Maie
made their principall feast to their god Vitzlipuztli, and two days before this feast, the
Virgins whereof I have spoken (the which were
shut up and secluded in the same temple and
were as it were religious women) did mingle a
quantitie of the seed of beetes with roasted Mays,
and then they did mould it with honie, making
an idoll of that paste in (likeness) bignesse like
to that of wood, putting insteade of eyes graines
of greene glasse, of blue, or white; and for teeth
graines of Mays set forth with all the ornament
and furniture that I have said. This being finished
all the noblemen came and brought it an ex-
quisite and rich garment, like unto that of the
idoll, wherewith they did attyre it. Being thus
clad and deckt, they did set it on an azured
chaire and in a litter to carry it on their shoulders.
The morning of this feast being come, an houre
before day all the maidens came forth attyred in
white with new ornaments, the which that day
were called the sisters of their god Vitzlipuztli,
they came crowned with garlands of Mays rosted

[ 31 ]

and parched, being like unto azahar or the flower of orange; and about their neckes they had great chaines of the same, which went bauldricke-wise under their left arm. Their cheeks were dyed with vermilion, their arms from elbow to the wrist were covered with red parrots' feathers. And thus attired they took the idol on their shoulders carrying it into the court, where all the yoong men were attired in garments of an artificial red, crowned after the same manner like unto the women. When as the maidens came forth with the idol the young men drew near with much reverence, taking the litter wherein the idol was, upon their shoulders, carrying it to the foot of the stairs of the Temple, where all the people did humble themselves, laying earth upon their heads, which was an ordinary ceremony which they did observe at the chief feast of their gods. This ceremony being ended, all the people went in procession with all the diligence and speed they could, going to a mountain, which was a league from the city of Mexico, called Chapultepec, and there they made sacrifices. Presently they went from thence with like diligence to go to a place near unto it which they called Atlacuyauaya, where they made their second station, and from thence they went

to another burgh or village a league beyond
Cuyoacan, from whence they parted, returning
to the city of Mexico, not making any other
station; they went in this sort above four leagues
in three or four hours, calling this procession
Ypayna Vitzlipuztli. Being come to the foote of
the stairs they set down the brankard or litter
with the idol, tying great cords to the arms of
the brankard; then with great observance and
reverence, they did draw up the litter with the
idol in it to the top of the Temple, some drawing
above and others helping below; in the meantime
there was a great noise of flutes, trumpets,
cornets and drums. They did mount it in this
manner, for that the stairs of the Temple were
very steep and narrow, so as they could not
carry up the litter upon their shoulders, while
they mounted up the idol all the people stood
in the court with much reverence and fear. Being
mounted to the top, and that they had placed it
in a little lodge of roses which they held ready,
presently came the young men, which strewed
many flowers of sundry kinds, wherein they
filled the Temple both within and without. This
done all the Virgins came out of their convent,
bringing pieces of paste compounded of beetes
and rosted Mays, which was of the same paste

whereof their idol was made and compounded, and they were of the fashion of great bones. They delivered them to the young men, who carried them up and laid them at the idol's feet, wherewith they filled the whole place that it could receive no more. They called these morcels of paste the flesh and bones of Vitzlipuztli. Having laid abroad these bones presently came all the Ancients of the Temple, Priests, Levites, and all the rest of the ministers, according to their dignities and antiquities (for herein there was a strict order amongst them) one after another, with their vailes of diverse colours and workes, every one according to his dignity and office, having garlands upon their heads and chains of flowers about their neckes; after them came their gods and goddesses whom they worshipt, of diverse figures, attyred in the same livery; then putting themselves in order about these morcels and pieces of paste, they used certain ceremonies with singing and dauncing. By meanes whereof they were dressed and consecrated for the flesh and bones of this idol.

This ceremony and blessing (whereby they were taken for the flesh and bones of the idol) being ended they honoured those pieces in the same sort as their god. Then came foorth the sacrificers, who began the sacrifice of men in the manner as hath beene spoken, and that day they did sacrifice a greater number than at any other time, for that it was the most solemn feast they observed. The sacrifices being ended all the yoong men and maides came out of the Temple attired as before, and being placed in order and rank, one directly against another, they daunced by drummes, the which sounded in praise of the feast, and of the idol which they did celebrate. To which song all the most ancient and greatest noble men did answer, dauncing about them, making a great circle, as their use is, the yoong men and maides remaining alwaies in the middest. All the citty came to this goodly spectacle, and there was a commaundment very strictly observed throughout all the land, that the day of the feast of the idol Vitzlipuztli they should eat no other meat but this paste, with hony, whereof the idol was made. And this should be eaten at the point of day, and they should drincke no water nor any other thing till after noon: they helde it for an ill signe, yea for sacrilege to doe the contrary: but after the ceremonies ended it was lawful to them to eat any thing. During the time of this ceremony they hid the water from their little children, admonishing all such as had the

[ 35 ]     3·2

use of reason not to drincke any water; which, if they did, the anger of God would come upon them, and they should die, which they did observe very carefully and strictly. The ceremonies, dancing, and sacrifice ended, they went to unclothe themselves, and the priests and superiors of the Temple took the idol of paste, which they spoiled of all the ornaments it had, and made many pieces as well of the idol itself as of the tronchons which were consecrated, and then they gave them to the people in manner of a communion, beginning with the greater, and continuing unto the rest, both men, women and little children, who received it with such tears, fear and reverence as it was an admirable thing, saying that they did eat the flesh and bones of God, wherewith they were grieved. Such as had any sick folks demanded thereof for them, and carried it with great reverence and veneration.

All such as did communicate were bound to give the tenth of this seed, whereof the idol was made. The solemnitie of the idol being ended an old man of great authoritie stepped up into a high place, and with a loud voice preached their law and ceremonies. Who would not wonder to see the devil so curious to seek to be worshipped and reverenced in the same way that Jesus Christ

[ 36 ]

our God hath appointed and also taught, and as the Holy Church hath accustomed. Hereby it is plainly verified what was propounded in the beginning, that Satan strives all he can to usurp and challenge unto himself the honour and service that is due to God alone, although he dooth still intermix with it his cruelties and filthiness, being the Spirit of murder and uncleanness and the father of lies.

In the third stage we are told that the use of dough or of a paste wafer has become so firmly established in the sacramental meal that it is no longer felt necessary to give them either animal or human shape. Again I give the extracts in full, taken from Fr. Acosta's account of Peruvian religious practices, and from other matter collected by Professor Jevons.

(1) That which is most admirable in the hatred and presumption of Sathan is that he hath not onely counfaited in idolatory and sacrifices but also in certain ceremonies our sacraments which Jesus Christ our Lord hath instituted and the Holy Church doth use, having especially pretended to imitate in some sort the sacrament of

the communion, which is the Most High and
Divine of all others, for the great error of Infidells
which proceeded in this manner. In the first
moneth, which in Peru they call Rayme and
answereth to our December, they made a most
solemn feast called Capacrayme wherein they
made many sacrifices and ceremonies, which continued many daies, during which no stranger
was suffered to bee at the court, which was in
Cusco. These days being past, they then gave
liberty to strangers to enter, that they might
be partakers of the feastes and sacrifices, minis-
tering to them in this manner. The Mamaconas
of the Sunne, which were a kind of Nuns of the
Sunne, made little loaves of the flower of Mays,
died and mingled with the blood of white sheep,
which they did sacrifice that day ; then presently
they commanded that all strangers should enter,
who set themselves in order; and the priests,
which were of a certain lineage descending from
the Luiquiyupangui, gave to every one a morcell
of these small loaves saying unto them that they
gave these pieces to the end that they should be
united and confederate with the Ynca, and that
they advised them not to speak nor think any ill
against the Ynca, but alwaies to beare him good
affection, for that this piece should be a witnesse

[ 38 ]

of their intentions and will, and if they did not as they ought he would discover them and be against them. They carried these small loaves in great platters of gold and silver appointed for that use, and all did receive and eat these pieces thanking the Sunne infinitely for so great a favour which he had done them, speaking words and making signes of great contentment and devotion; protesting that during their lives they would neither do nor think any thing against the Sunne nor the Ynca: and with this condition they received this foode of the Sunne, the which remains in their bodies for a witness of their fidelitie which they observed to the Sunne and to the Ynca their king. This manner of divelish communicating they likewise used in the 10th month called Coyarayme, which was September, in the solemn feast they call Cytua, doing the like ceremonies. And besides this communion (if it be lawful to use the word in so divelish a matter) which they imparted to all strangers that came, they did likewise send of these loaves to all their guacas, santuaries, or idolls of the whole Realme; and at one instant they found people of all sides which came expressly to receive them, to whom they said (in delivering them) that the Sunne had sent them that in signe that hee would have them all to

LOCALISATION IN FOOD

worship and honour (and) him, and likewise did
send them in honour of the Caciques. Some per-
happes will hold this for a fable and a fiction;
yet it is most true that, since the Ynca Yupangi
(the which is hee that hath made most laws,
customs, and ceremonies, as Numa did in Rome),
this manner of communion hath continued untill
the gospel of Our Lord Jesus Christ thrust out
all these superstitions giving them the right foode
of life, which united their soules to God. Whoso
would satisfie himselfe more amply let him reade
the relation which the Licentiate Polo did write
to Don Jeronimo de Loaysa, Archbishop of the
Cittie of Kings, where he shall find this and
many other things which he hath discovered
and found out by his great dilligence.

(2) Thus in the New World[1] annually among
the Mayas, consecrated wafers were broken, dis-
tributed, and preserved as a protection against
misfortune for the year. In Peru, in August,
four sheep were offered to four divinities, and
"when this sacrifice was offered up, the priest
had the sancu ("a pudding of coarsely ground
maize") on great plates of gold, and he sprinkled
it with the blood of the sheep....The high priest
then said in a loud voice, so that all might hear:

[1] Jevons, *op. cit.*

"Take heed how you eat this sancu; for he who eats it in sin, and with a double will and heart, is seen by our father the Sun, who will punish him with grievous troubles. But he who with a single heart partakes of it, to him the Sun and the Thunder will show favour, and will grant children, and happy years and abundance, and all that he requires." Then they all rose up to partake, first making a solemn vow, before eating the yahuar-sancu ("yahuar"—blood, "sancu"—pudding), in which they promised never to murmur against the Creator, the Sun or the Thunder; never to be traitors to their lord the Ynca, on pain of receiving condemnation and trouble. The priest of the Sun then took what he could hold on three fingers, put it into his mouth and then returned to his seat. In this order and in this manner of taking the oath all the tribes rose up and thus all partook, down to the little children....They took it with such care that no particle was allowed to fall to the ground, this being looked upon as a great sin.

It is noticeable that the practices described were common among the peoples of the ancient central American civilisation, which, from whatever source it may have derived, grew up admittedly to its full flowering in isolation from that of other parts of the world. It is curious to notice how the Jesuit fathers employ precisely the same language as Justin and Tertullian in their endeavour to account for the existence of sacramental rites among non-Christians. I will conclude with two more extracts from Jevons.

(1) ..............................we find these consecrated cakes associated, amongst the ancient Prussians, with the rite—which we have already quoted as a typical instance of the sacrificial meal. Whilst the flesh of the animal victim was cooking, rye-cakes were made and were baked, not in an oven, but by being continually tossed over the fire by the men standing round, who threw them and caught them. These consecrated wafers survive also in "Beltane cakes." These cakes are made on the evening before Beltane, May 1 (O.S.); in Ross-shire they are called "tcharnican," i.e. "hand-cake," because they are made wholly in the hand (not on a board or table like common cakes) and are not to be put on any table or dish; they must never be put from the hand—like the Peruvian "sancu," to allow which to fall from the hand was a great sin.

(2) In the Old World the use of wafers or cakes not in human or animal shape has not left many traces. In Tartary they were used, as one eye-witness, Father Grueber, testifies: "This only do I affirm, that the devil so mimics the Catholic Church there, that although no European or Christian has ever been there, still in all essential things they agree so completely with the Roman Church as even to celebrate the sacrifice of the Host with bread and wine: with my own eyes have I seen it."

It is perfectly clear that the divine presence was believed to be in some way locally mediated to the recipient by these various kinds of food which were therefore treated with reverence and veneration.

## THE EUCHARISTIC PRESENCE

I have quoted the foregoing passages, not of course in order to belittle the Christian sacrament, but in order to point out the fact that the mechanism (so to speak) of the sacramental meal and of the veneration of food is the same outside Christianity as it is inside it. The difference lies in the character of the Deity whose presence is in each case mediated to the worshipper rather than in the mechanism of the mediation. It is necessary therefore to consider a little the alleged nature of this local sacramental presence.

The late Dr Rashdall once defined the locality of the divine action by saying: "A spirit is where it acts." Taken in relation to a sacrament or image this definition plainly localises the divine presence in the occasion when a material substance is used, rather than in the substance itself, whether bread, wine, salt, oil, wood, stone or the like. There is a very famous passage in Cardinal Newman's "Via media" in which he seems to adopt this view: "If place is excluded from the idea of the sacramental presence, then division or distance from heaven is excluded also....Moreover if the idea of distance is excluded, therefore is the idea of motion. Our Lord then neither descends from heaven upon our altars, nor moves when carried in procession. The visible species change their position but he does not move. He is in the Holy Eucharist after the manner of a spirit."

This view, which almost any reasonable person would be glad to accept, is not the language of sanctioned popular devotion[1], nor is it plainly taught by the majority of Catholic theologians, although there are some who, as Bishop Gore says: "Allow to the consecrated bread and wine all the reality which anyone believes any bread and wine to possess, or in other words explain away transubstantiation till it remains little more than a verbal incumbrance due to an inopportune intrusion into church doctrine of a temporary phase of metaphysics[2]."

The well-known Roman Catholic Bishop of Newport, Dr Hedley, has aimed at showing by the usual catena of evidence that there

---

[1] "My Good Jesus! I am about to have the joy of receiving You into my heart. The little white Host which the priest will give me under the form of bread is You, my adorable Jesus! You hide Yourself that You may come down to me." (From a Roman Catholic book of devotion for children issued in 1913 with the imprimatur of the R.C. Bishop of Nottingham.)

[2] *The Body of Christ.*

was a very early belief on the part of Christians that in the sacramental bread and wine there was localised by consecration a definite divine essence, and that there was a clear belief that in the Eucharist there was dominical sanction for such a unique association of the Deity with material food that the word idolatry did not apply to the reverence with which it was regarded.

I do not think Bishop Hedley has shown how this early belief arose, and I do not think that we are even now able to show precisely in what way it developed, but of this I am certain, that the evidence shows us that it was a genuine development and not something which was there from the outset.

The first thing to remember is that we are at this point dealing not with dogmatic theory but with indisputable religious experience. Probably the earliest type of this experience is recorded for us in the story of the journey of the two disciples to Emmaus in which the words occur: "He was known

unto them in the breaking of the bread."
We may well believe that such an experience accompanied the breakings of bread
which we find according to the narrative of
Acts to have been of frequent occurrence.
In it the disciples felt themselves to be the
"commensales" of their invisible Lord. A
similar reference may possibly be found in
the passage of the Fourth Gospel where we
read that Jesus came and stood in the midst
of the disciples and said: "Peace be unto
you." But this solemn participation of food
and drink naturally excited the thought and
stimulated the speculation of the Christian.
Living as he did in a world where educated
persons were greatly influenced by the Platonic tradition, he tended to think of the
things that happened in the flesh as being
likenesses, copies, or types of the realities
which existed in the heavenly world. The
effects of this can be seen in the fragments
of Christian public prayer which have been
preserved to us. In the primitive Communion
prayer of the Didache we have, as Bishop

Gore admits, a representation of the Eucharist as "a social meal charged with the breath of mysticism." It was in fact a social meal of the "Emmaus" type. There was however another view of the Eucharist in which the presence of the Lord was more closely associated with the actual consecrated food. Thus we read in Irenaeus (c. 180 A.D.): "The bread which is of the earth receiving the invocation of God is no longer common bread but Eucharist made up of two things, an earthly and a heavenly." In Justin Martyr (a little earlier) occurs the familiar passage: "This food is called by us Eucharist...for not as common bread and common drink do we receive these but like as Jesus Christ our Saviour being made flesh through the word of God took both flesh and blood for our salvation, so also were we taught that the food for which thanks are given by the word of prayer that comes from him, food by which blood and flesh by conversion are nourished, is both flesh and blood of that Jesus who was made flesh." In the prayer of the Egyptian

[ 48 ]

Bishop Sarapion which is dated at about 350 we find the combination of both lines of thought. The Bishop combines a prayer of Didache type with one in which an invocation of the Word of God is called over the food; nevertheless he expressly declares that the bread and the cup are only the "likeness" (ὁμοίωμα) of the body and the blood. In the "Testamentum domini" (dated between 375 and 475) we read: "The cup of wine which He mixed He gave for a type of the blood." A consecration prayer[1] attributed to St Gregory Nazianzen says: "Of this my freedom I offer to Thee the symbols and ascribe to Thy words that which is accomplished for Thou art He who didst commit to me this mystic participation of Thy flesh in bread and wine." St Cyril of Jerusalem, who is almost if not quite the first to speak of the bread and wine as being actually "changed by consecration," retains this old Platonic phraseology when he says: " In the figure of

---

[1] For this and other extracts see Linton, *Twenty-five Consecration prayers*. S.P.C.K. 1921.

bread is given thee the body and in the figure of wine is given the blood." The identification of the symbol (charged with associations) with the reality symbolised is evidently at present incomplete. Transubstantiatory language is accompanied by other phrases of a more figurative character. Thus Theodoret (fifth cent.) says: "The bread and the wine do not depart from their proper nature; for they remain in their former substance and shape and form." When however we come to the year 750 we find St John Damascene definitely refusing to allow the elements after consecration to be called types or symbols of the body and blood, since consecration effects a fundamental change in them. Whereas the earlier fathers "escaped the perils of localisation by a rich variety of language[1]," in proportion as church theology and devotional piety develop we arrive at the result that the East adopts a belief in a change which identifies the symbol with the reality and openly expresses the belief in appropriate

[1] Bp Gore in *The Body of Christ*.

language, while the West also uniformly adopts the belief but retains conservative language in its forms of devotion, as may be seen from the Canon of the Roman Mass[1].

To what was this momentous result due? It would appear to have been due, not merely to the attempt to give an account of Christian experience, but also to the twofold effect of (1) primitive exegesis of the New Testament and (2) pressure from without of Gentile beliefs concerning the nature of consecrated food, of the kind of which we have already given examples.

The study of the New Testament led to an elucidation of the words of institution such as we find in Cyril of Jerusalem[2] who says: "Surely He who could turn water into wine can if He so wills turn bread and wine into His body and blood." Further exposition of Gentile beliefs seems at this point unnecessary.

[1] I desire to acknowledge some helpful suggestions in this section which I have received from the Rev. E. C. Ratcliff, Vice-Principal of Westcott House.

[2] Cyril, *Scr. Cat. Myst.* iv. 2.

Modern students naturally feel that the interpretation of Eucharistic experience must at any rate to some extent be determined by a consideration of the philosophical fitness of the conception of a presence localised in the elements and also by our knowledge of the contemporary thought of Judaism in the circles in which Christ moved and taught, and of the general trend of His own teaching. An additional problem presents itself when the practice arises of reserving the sacramental elements not merely for extended communion but for actual veneration.

The conception of the relation of space to Deity comes first. If we regard God as extended in space, does His universal extension preclude His local action? Cannot man covenant with Him to receive from Him the benefits of intercourse at an individual point? It must surely be admitted that if in any real sense we accept the incarnation of Deity in the historical Jesus as unique we thereby conceive the local action of the Deity in any experience in which the presence of Christ is associated with our performance of a sacramental act.

Nevertheless we are somewhat impeded in our clear apprehension of the present relation to space-time of the Divine Christ in the Godhead by the persistence both in Anglican and in Roman formularies of the obsolete description of Heaven as a place and not as a state or mode of existence. (R. C. Catechism, resp. 70, and the Black Rubric, B. C. P.: Dec. Trent. Conc. sess. xiii. c. 1 says however that "Christ is in heaven according to the natural *mode* of existence," which is ambiguous.)

With regard to the general background to the teaching of our Lord and to His own teaching the most that we can say is that the facts are neutral. Of the fanatical opposition to idolatry, traceable in Acts and known to have been intensified by the misdeeds of Antiochus Epiphanes,—of this there is truly not a single trace in the Gospels. Jesus neither condemns nor licenses localisation. He is humanly speaking Quaker in His attitude to the world around, tolerant alike of John's baptism and of the temple sacrifices, but tied and limited by neither. We are entitled I think to infer that He would have regarded with tolerance the psychological make-up of so many human beings which prevents them from apprehending the spiritual presence of God or of appropriating His gifts save through sacramental emblems, but we are scarcely justified in assuming that He did not mean to build the main super-structure of His permanent message upon the solid foundation of Jewish monotheism with its dislike of symbols.

## COMPARATIVE RELIGION AGAIN

Let us return again for a little to the primitives and ask "What is a sacred object?" Some things are sacred, others not; some things are specially connected with God, others are not. Further, there are degrees of reverence due to sacred things. Only some of these things are treated with actual "puja[1]."

---

[1] A crucifix, a palm, or a picture may be sacred, not because of any Divine indwelling consciously believed

But what is intended when it is said that the Deity is connected with a certain object? Primitive man evidently thought of the connection as akin to the charging of the substance with electricity. The charge in many cases is almost negligible, but when intensified it becomes powerful in its effects and even dangerous. This possession of a divine power by a sacred object would be due

in, but because they *remind* us of Christ. I have record of a Masonic procession held in a London church in which a Bible was ceremonially carried on a cushion by four boys. This however would only be "relative honour." When however may we say that the Rubicon has been crossed? Robert Dale of Birmingham, in his sermon on the Second Commandment, tells how he removed a picture of Christ from his sitting-room because he found himself developing an inability to pray fervently without regarding it, and he desired to avoid becoming dependent on it for help in concentration.

I am not sure that I feel secure about Prof. Percy Gardner's distinction between "lower and higher idolatry" which I have just seen (*Mod. Churchman*, April, 1928, p. 18), in spite of his persuasive quotation from Maximus Tyrius. Of course it is better to have a beautiful than a repulsive icon. But that doesn't settle the question as to whether localisation is wrong or not. In any case the cult of the tabernacle is not "barbarous and uncouth." If it *is* wrong, it must be wrong for some other reason.

to various causes and a description of these is just a rationalisation of a process perceived rather than understood. The primitive judges by the result, and seeks to interpret it accordingly. He dares not underestimate the effects which he feels to be mighty. He therefore says the God is *in* the object. Localisation is in fact simply one explanation of the way in which the use of the object is effectual. The sacredness may be due to (1) sound, as in the case of the bullroarer, the cymbals, the drum, or the sistrum, (2) size or shape, especially if peculiar or impressive, (3) unfamiliarity, e.g. a mountain to people who have never seen one before, (4) associated ideas, especially if seeing an object recalls circumstances originally charged with emotion.

The sacredness of the Eucharistic elements would appear to be of the last order. In the first instance the sight of the Eucharistic bread and cup (of such a type for example as may be seen in the Catacomb paintings) would recall the occasions when the Christian disciples were the "commensales" of their divine Lord. It would not be difficult to make a rationalisation of such an impression by saying practically what Justin Martyr has done in the well-known passage which we have quoted, and we have seen that from this it is an easy step to regarding the elements as, not merely types or figures in a drama in which the Lord is mystically present (just as He had been present in the flesh at the Last Supper), but as actually charged or suffused with divine spirit, so that whether touched, eaten, or gazed at, they are capable of influencing profoundly the individual who so comes into contact with them. There is no need to deny Christian experience, but we are not bound to accept blindly all the attempts which have been made at relating the consecrated elements to that experience.

### CATHOLICISM AND HINDUISM

Attention may well be drawn at this point to the consistent devotional practice of the learned Roman Catholic Modernist, Baron Friedrich von Hügel, in whose life the practice of a daily visit to the Carmelite Church at Kensington in order to pray before the Tabernacle co-existed with the profession of a definitely liberal theology. Such a combination strangely resembles what we find in India. The educated Hindu not only tolerates localisation in cultus on the part of his unsophisticated neighbours, but not infrequently indulges in it himself. Probably many of us will remember Sir Alfred Lyall's description of the Hindu officer[1]:

Of great shrewdness and very fair education... who devoted several hours daily to the elaborate worship of five round pebbles which he had appointed to be his symbol of Omnipotence.

Sankara, a quotation from whom I have put at the head of my essay, in spite of his own Puritan sentiments, did not forbid localisation to his followers. Thus it is recorded

[1] Quoted by J. B. Pratt, *The Religious Consciousness.*

of one ascetic of his group, that he said of his food-bowl, "that is Brahma," and when questioned added[1]:

Brahma dwells in it temporarily, but name and form pass...name and form pass, but the eternal abides.

One intelligent Hindu said to Professor Pratt[1]:

The image is not Shiva. Shiva is in Heaven, but I want to worship him, so I make a picture or image as like him in appearance as I can, and then I pray to Shiva in front of it because it helps me to pray.

This statement naturally reminds us of certain women in the western province of China, Sze-Chuan, who said that they were quite unable to understand how people could pray "unless they had a god in the room." A learned Bengali Brahmin said to Professor Pratt that he retained image-cultus explicitly for its psychological effects[1]:

"The idol," he said, "is useful in aiding visualisation and concentration. It is a sensuous symbol,

[1] J. B. Pratt, *India and its Faiths*.

like the word G-O-D. Both are symbols, one tangible and visible, the other audible; and both are helpful to our finite minds in standing before the Infinite."

It is to be noted that the earliest use of images in India seems to have been connected with the worship of the one Vedic deity who was invisible—Indra. There can be no doubt that India to-day provides us with the doughtiest and ablest defenders of localisation, and those who study religious psychology are not slow to recognise this, although they may not all agree with the arguments used. Thus, for example, Professor Pratt describes the cultus of the sacred lingam in a shrine of Mahadev by a Hindu widow and adds[1]:

Repugnant as idolatry seems to us, there can be no doubt that as a fact this Hindu widow, and many like her, finds a reinforcement for her faith in the sensuous presence of a physical object,—a reinforcement of faith which she at any rate, being what she is, could not find without it. Doubtless the "Great God," Mahadev,

[1] Pratt, *The Religious Consciousness.*

is present everywhere; but what is that abstract doctrine compared to the sense of the closeness of the deity and to the realisation of his presence which come to the poor soul when she sees the sacred symbol of the mystery of life directly before her, and when she pours her offering and lays her flowers upon this concrete object in which the Great God has consented, for the moment and for her sake, to take up his miraculous abode?

It is interesting to set side by side with this an observation of the famous Indian Christian Sadhu Sundar Singh who, so far from being a Catholic, owes his Christianity to Presbyterian influence. When however his attention was drawn to the use of the Tabernacle by one of his Anglo-Catholic friends, he said[1]:

I have no objection to idolatry if it serves as a means of bringing men to Christ, and if it makes mental concentration and prayer easier.

The Sadhu here I think betrays his Hindu ancestry, and it is worth noting that he frankly refers to the cultus of the reserved

[1] Quoted in Heiler's *Biography of the Sadhu.*

[ 61 ]

sacrament as idolatry. It never occurs to him apparently that this description is likely to cause offence, or that it is unjust or inaccurate.

Professor Pratt says that the Parsees are sometimes spoken of as fire-worshippers, and adds that this is an ignorant calumny, since Parsees are no more fire-worshippers than Christians are bread and wine worshippers[1]:

The Parsee may pray anywhere; but he prays best in the presence of some sort of fire, the supreme symbol, to him, of the Eternal God.

Pratt's own views are sympathetically expressed in his two principal books, and may be summarised as follows. Much more may be said in defence of the practice of idolatry than most of us have been brought up to suppose. It is based upon a perfectly sound psychological principle, and it appeals to a widely felt human need. Nevertheless Pratt is no advocate of idolatry, for while he admits that it has certain decided psychological advantages, he thinks that with equal

Pratt, *India and its Faiths.*

certainty it introduces certain grave dangers.
It makes religion easy, and sometimes cheap,
for while the use of images renders it easier
for the mind to realise the presence of the
Divine, it is questionable whether the
Divine does not lose more of excellence in
the process than it gains in power. In localisation the Divine is dwarfed in order to be
made assimilable to the human mind without stretching the latter ; as if the stretching
of the mind were not one of the chief ser-
vices which religion does for man. The
danger of images lies in the ease of their
misuse, and in India the great majority of
those who use them misuse them.

An entirely different view is that of the
Esthonian philosopher Count Hermann
Keyserling. The curious adaptability of his
temperament, and his tendency to idealise
everything he sees render him a witness
whose evidence must be received with cau-
tion. He is, however, I believe, correct in
saying that the spirit of Hinduism, regarded
as a cohesion of religious ideas and forms,

[ 63 ]

is identical with that of Catholicism, only
the spirit seems in the case of the former
to be more intellectualised. Perhaps it is best
to quote the whole passage :

The practical regulations which are prescribed
to the faithful of both religions have the same
significance everywhere, they are equally wise,
equally profound psychologically, equally to the
purpose. Only the Hindus have understood the
same thing in a better way. Thus, the Catholic
Church recommends the veneration of saints
because the saints are really supposed to abide
in heaven, really act as advocates before God,
who is believed to have arranged that we are not
to approach him directly, but to address ourselves to the appropriate intermediaries; the
Indians know that the devotion to specified
divinities is advisable, because it is too difficult
for men to realise divinity as such, because
realisation is the one and only thing on which
everything depends, and because a specific form
appropriate to specific aspirations is most beneficial. Catholicism as well as Hinduism worships
images; but whereas in practice it is only too
often a question of real fetishism, idol-worship
in its crudest form, for the Catholic, every Hindu

[ 64 ]

knows (or can know it at any rate) that the value
of images depends solely on the fact that they
help to concentrate the attention of the praying
individual; it is impossible for most people to
concentrate their souls except in reference to a
visible object, and so forth. In the Catholic
Church the profound doctrines of antiquity con-
tinue to exist in a misrepresented form; within
Hinduism they are generally interpreted correctly. So far as the principle is in question, this
is the only difference between the two religions.

It is probable that most of us will react
violently against this statement of Keyserling's; but we must remember that he is
speaking of the regulation of piety rather
than of dogma.

Two other passages may be quoted to
illustrate his point of view, both taken from
the part of his diary which relates his visit
to Benares.

(1) During these days, in which I have wit-
nessed so many cults, I have become more con-
scious than ever how much the development
of humanity tends away from ritualism; magic
loses more and more in meaning and purpose.
To this extent the world tends undoubtedly to-

wards Protestantism. Fewer and fewer cultured
Hindus follow the prescriptions of the Tantras
accurately; the Catholic Church lays less and
less stress upon the help we are to find in ritual.
Apparently it is less and less effective. Ever
since the 18th century Catholicism in Europe
does not achieve what, theoretically, it could
and should achieve, and it seems to-day as if its
profession did more harm than good in general.
Why? The explanation is surely not that the
Tantras do not embody anything but supersti-
tion, that what was always the case is only
being recognised now, nor is the position, as the
theosophists assert, that modern humanity is
forfeiting one of the most important means to
salvation; and it is quite certain that the cessation
of belief in magic as effective does not cover the
ultimate cause of the situation. I personally am
convinced that the teachings of the Tantras are
correct on the whole, and that it is nevertheless
true that they meet with less and less observance.
Magic can only be effective where consciousness
is in a certain position; this position can only be
maintained in a certain equilibrium of psychic
forces, in which critical intelligence does not
disturb the creations of imagination and faith.
Where this necessary equilibrium exists, magic

is, of course, efficacious; and in those cases Tantric ceremonies often imply the safest means to inner progress. But where this equilibrium is disturbed, their effect is nil. And it is disturbed in the whole of humanity more and more in the sense that the intellect outweighs imagination. This induces progress everywhere where mastery of the external world is in question; but it involves simultaneously losing out of sight another side of reality. The man who is beyond the Tantra stage is superior to many influences of the psychic sphere which are often disturbing, but he also misses their positive qualities. Supreme self-realisation is within reach of the one as much as the other; he is, moreover, much better fitted to understand it. Whereas the Tantrika generally interprets real experiences in the light of absurd theories, the man of clear understanding is in a position to interpret objectively and correctly. But he is aware of it much more rarely. There is no doubt that the soul of the Tantrika is open to influences which do not react upon any other condition of consciousness at all; and no doubt the process of growing beyond this state implies a loss. We Europeans with our clear intellect do not experience a great deal of that which the superstitious Hindu experiences.

## CATHOLICISM AND HINDUISM

(2) The Indians who have gone farther in self-recognition than any other men, whose consciousness has freed itself to an incredible degree from the entangled fetters of names and forms, have always been Catholic in practice; all the greatest Indian philosophers like Ramanuja, Shankaracharia—I have said it already—practised just like Thomas Aquinas. There have, of course, been reformers with Protestant tendencies among Indians, as everywhere else, as, for instance, Buddha, the Gurus of the Sikhs, and lately the founders of Brahmo-Samaj. But to begin with not one of them has gone as far as Luther did among us, and then they were never able to conquer the Hindu spirit on a great scale; they never became popular. Buddhism disappeared from India as soon as it lost the external support of regal power, and the other Protestant religions have all remained limited sects. What does this mean? It means that, in view of the Hindus, Catholicism embodies a system of mental hygiene which could not conceivably have been improved upon; that, whatever the ultimate meaning of religion may be, the Catholic form conduces best to its realisation. The most essential technical feature of all Protestant reforms is that they have simplified the apparatus which serves spiritual

progress. Whereas Catholicism employs every means which seems calculated to stimulate religious feeling, Protestantism sanctions only a few and impresses upon the soul to enter into relation with God, in all simplicity and candour, without external assistance. This would be all very well if communion with God could be attained by this less circuitous route with the same degree of perfection. This is the point on which the Hindus differ. According to their experience, only the highest man has the inner right to choose the path of Protestantism, for he alone can hope to find God in seeking him in his own way. The others do not find him. For them it is better to avail themselves of the whole apparatus of assistance which the wisdom of generations has developed, and to travel along the broad road which it has marked out for all.

It would be mistaken to put the question as to whether the Hindus are absolutely right in their attitude; undoubtedly they are right for themselves. The roads of Catholicism and Protestantism both lead to God, but each one of them is appropriate to special natures.

However much we may dislike facing facts, it seems to me impossible to evade this final conclusion of Keyserling. Setting on one side for the moment what he says about the simplification effected by Protestantism, it seems to me that the tendency of modern education is, exactly as Keyserling says, "to disturb equilibrium." Modern man is intrinsically an intellectual being. Only that which he has *understood* becomes a vital force to him. The problem is to make the intellect more profound, since, once it has developed sufficiently to understand the meaning of faith and the deep significance of what it has come with shallow observation to regard as nonsense, it will then become once more religious.

It is only fair to set side by side with the observations of Pratt and Keyserling the evidence of Protestant missionaries of the enlightened type, since these are actually closer and more continuously in contact with Hinduism as a working system. First it must be noted that they draw attention to the process by which localisation is effected. It would seem that we have here among Hindus two co-existent but mutually inconsistent modes of thought. While, on the one hand, it is believed that the deity is present everywhere within external objects, and localisation involves little more than attention in space-time focussed upon an omnipresent reality, on the other hand no image is considered a proper object for worship until it has been consecrated. The consecration must be performed by a priest, not by anyone, and it involves the performance of a definite ceremony in which certain sacred words are spoken. The whole ceremony is described by a term which, being translated, means "quickening" or bringing the life of the god into the image, and it is in principle precisely the same as that in which the Eucharistic elements are consecrated by a Catholic priest. It is true, as we have seen, that educated Hindus will repudiate this notion of special presence and will declare that the idol is only a symbol, but the Hindu peasants at least, if not many Hindus of better education, regard their images as though they possessed a kind of

electric charge. The Rev. W. E. S. Holland
gives it as his experience that:

the most deadly issue of idolatry is seen in the
incapacity of even the more educated members
of the race (so gifted for abstract thought) to
conceive God in prayer apart from some definite
shape and form...if idolatry is an education de-
signed gradually to lead simple people to a more
spiritual worship, it has not in all these ages got
its pupils beyond the infant classes[1].

## THE SACRAMENTS IN THEORY

The claim is made that the Eucharistic
elements are in a different category from any
other material elements used in religious
worship. It is held that the words of institution used by Christ at the Last Supper,
whether they be employed in the actual
prayer of consecration or no, define the
nature of the consecrated elements in such

[1] *The Goal of India*, p. 54. One gifted young missionary
recently returned on furlough insists strongly on the fact
that the Hindus themselves make very little distinction
between their cultus and that of the Roman Catholics
in India, and seem to think of Catholicism rather as
a branch of Hinduism.

a way that they are lifted altogether into another region of being. Eucharistic adoration is therefore not the latreia of something material nor even the cultus of an ordinary image, but something more—not so much the overthrowing of a sacrament, as the apotheosis of a sacrament. But, as I think I have shown, this belief in a presence localised in the elements obviously resembles that claimed as existing between sacred food and deities in other religions and it may well be argued that this is indeed a case of Christianity accepting a religious theory previously found elsewhere. Food offered in sacrifice is, as we have seen, held after consecration to be transubstantiated or suffused with *mana*, "*ἀρετή*," or *virtus*, or whatever else is the description of the divine energy.

We have seen that this adoption was a genuine development due to certain causes; but we are not bound to the necessity of supposing that the simple ordinance of Jesus was ever consciously intended to be assimilated to ordinary Gentile sacramental practice. It was perhaps inevitable under the circumstances that it should become so assimilated. The temptation to make an unconscious treaty with natural religion in the interests of mass-conversion was irresistible. But this does not mean that he who first ordained the κυρίακον δεῖπνον accepted the theory of a localisation in food of some divine essence which he believed to be part of himself. If he did then I submit that it would be legitimate to parody the words of the Lady Margaret Professor at Oxford and to describe the religion founded by Jesus Christ as "entitled to call itself— with pride and not with apology—by divine appointment the supreme and ideal form of idolatry[1]." This is after all what the champions of Catholic devotion have done. They have not only said that since the Incarnation a certain degree of localised προσκύνησις has been sanctioned, but they have also declared that the Blessed Sacrament may be treated with λατρεία because "it is God himself."

[1] See *Essays Catholic and Critical*, p. 396.

[ 74 ]

I venture to suggest that on the basis of Dean Rashdall's definition the only occasion when it is possible to regard a change as occurring in a material substance is when by its special arrangement it becomes charged or invested with a meaning or use which in its raw or unarranged condition it did not possess. Thus printer's ink when arranged in certain shapes on a white piece of paper is capable of conveying ideas which were not conveyable by the ink in the bottle. It has become the vehicle of meaning and is now capable of exciting emotion, imparting mental concepts and information, and inciting to action. Yet the printer's ink remains—to use the phrase—in its natural substance. Now so long as any material object is recognised as remaining in its natural substance, there can be no harm in using it as the vehicle of meaning. The harm only occurs when the acquisition of meaning is believed to alter the atomic structure or composition of the material object. In a recent defence of Catholic devotion the present Master of Corpus

[ 75 ]

Christi College, Cambridge[1], has given us two
other examples of the use of material objects
charged with meaning. A sacrament, he says,
is an effectual symbol because it not merely
conveys a message but also effects a result,
and he quotes the use of the sword in the
accolade, and the use of money in purchase,
and he remarks with regard to the latter:
"those who recognise the authority which
appoints the token do not in fact use or think
of their florins as counters." The elements
of a religious sacrament differ only from
these other symbols in that the results and
opportunities of experience which they
effect and bring are determined by the
authority of God Himself. This is a perfectly
fair position to adopt *so long as the acquisition
of meaning and effectiveness is not believed to
alter the atomic structure or composition of the
material object,* for the florin, whatever pur-
chasing power it may convey, remains a
counter.

It is to be noted that so far as the Christian

[1] See *Essays Catholic and Critical,* p. 429.

[ 76 ]

sacraments are concerned the water of baptism has usually been regarded in this way.
Instances of a belief in the alteration of its
atomic structure as the result of consecration
are rare. The water of baptism is like the
ink on a cheque (a series of drops of ink
charged with meaning); but the water itself remains unchanged; it has no difference
from other specimens of water, rendering
it of medicinal or surgical value, unless its
power of suggestion in the case of superstitious persons be taken into account. Yet all
would hold the latter to be a perversion of
the proper function of the water of baptism
even if the result achieved were a faith cure.

Similarly the bread and wine of the Eucharist become, by any form of consecratory
prayer, charged with meaning. They become
effective instruments in conveying whatever
gift Christ intended to convey to His followers by them. It is extremely doubtful,
however, whether they were meant by Him
to be used as localised centres for purposes
of concentration apart from the communal

meal. That the consecrated bread has so come to be used is I think a matter for no surprise in view of the considerations which have gone before. It is noticeable that reservation for the purpose of exposition, adoration, or benediction is normally in one kind only and not in two. It is obvious that the essential point is that there should be something definite and easy to see, the round white disc of the Host or at least the white curtain in front of the tabernacle. The general agreement of Catholic Christians to use this object as a means of concentration is not difficult to appreciate, charged as it is with so many intense and sacred memories, and those who have practised devotions in front of it especially in Continental churches have told me that even on the acceptance of only such a theory of a sacramental element as I have just set forth they have felt, as they have put it, that "there was Something or Someone on the other side of the symbol." I would advise anyone to read Mgr Benson's story "In the

Convent Chapel" published in his volume *The Light Invisible*, a book which was written before he became a Roman Catholic, and from which I quote the following passage —which I believe to be autobiographical:

"I became aware, in my intellect alone, of one or two clear facts. In order to tell you what those facts were I must use picture language; but remember they are only translations or paraphrases of what I perceived.

"First I became aware suddenly that there ran a vital connection from the Tabernacle to the woman. You may think of it as one of those bands you see in machinery connecting two wheels, so that when either wheel moves the other moves too. Or you may think of it as an electric wire, joining the instrument the telegraph operator uses with the pointer at the other end. At any rate there was this vital band or wire of life.

"Now in the Tabernacle I became aware that there was a mighty stirring and movement. Something within it beat like a vast Heart, and the vibrations of each pulse seemed to quiver through all the ground. Or you may picture it as the movement of a clear deep pool when the basin that contains it is jarred—it seemed like the

movement of circular ripples crossing and re-
crossing in swift thrills. Or you may think of it
as that faint movement of light and shade that
may be seen in the heart of a white-hot furnace.
Or again you may picture it as sound—as the
sound of a high ship-mast with the rigging, in
a steady wind; or the sound of deep woods in a
July noon."

The priest's face was working, and his hands
moved nervously.

"How hopeless it is," he said, "to express all
this! Remember that all these pictures are not
in the least what I perceived. They are only
grotesque paraphrases of a spiritual fact that was
shown me.

"Now I was aware that there was something of
the same activity in the heart of the woman, but
I did not know which was the controlling power.
I did not know whether the initiative sprang from
the Tabernacle and communicated itself to the
nun's will; or whether she, by bending herself
upon the Tabernacle, set in motion a huge dor-
mant power. It appeared to me possible that the
solution lay in the fact that two wills co-operated,
each reacting upon the other. This, in a kind of
way, appears to me now true as regards the whole
mystery of free-will and prayer and grace.

"At any rate the union of these two represented itself to me, as I have said, as forming a kind of engine that radiated an immense light or sound or movement. And then I perceived something else too.

"I once fell asleep in one of those fast trains from the north, and did not awake until we had reached the terminus. The last thing I had seen before falling asleep had been the quiet darkening woods and fields through which we were sliding, and it was a shock to awake in the bright humming terminus and to drive through the crowded streets, under the electric glare from the lamps and windows. Now I felt something of that sort now. A moment ago I had fancied myself apart from movement and activity in this quiet convent; but I seemed somehow to have stepped into a centre of busy, rushing life. I can scarcely put the sensation more clearly than that. I was aware that the atmosphere was charged with energy; great powers seemed to be astir, and I to be close to the whirling centre of it all.

"Or think of it like this. Have you ever had to wait in a City office? If you have done that you will know how intense quiet can coexist with intense activity. There are quiet figures here and there round the room. Or it may be there is only one such figure—a great financier—and he sitting there almost motionless. Yet you know that every movement tingles, as it were, out from that still room all over the world. You can picture to yourself how people leap to obey or to resist—how lives rise and fall, and fortunes are made and lost, at the gentle movements of this lonely quiet man in his office. Well, so it was here. I perceived that this black figure knelt at the centre of reality and force, and with the movements of her will and lips controlled spiritual destinies for eternity. There ran out from this peaceful chapel lines of spiritual power that lost themselves in the distance, bewildering in their profusion and terrible in the intensity of their hidden fire. Souls leaped up and renewed the conflict as this tense will strove for them. Souls, even at that moment leaving the body, struggled from death into spiritual life, and fell panting and saved at the feet of the Redeemer on the other side of death. Others, acquiescent and swooning in sin, woke and snarled at the merciful stab of this poor nun's prayers."

Except for the character of the Deity "on the other side" I cannot for the life of me see how these experiences differ as far as the mechanism of them goes from those of the properly taught Hindu who uses a localised symbol. Indeed so long as the language of the Catholic pratiquant only involves that the elements *mean* the presence of Christ in the sense that G-O-D *means* the Deity it is hard to see any serious objection in a localised cultus. It may be said that to concentrate locally on a consecrated wafer in order to perceive the omnipresent spirit may be arbitrary, since it would be quite as reasonable to concentrate upon the figure of Christ whether depicted in a stained glass window or projected on to a sheet by a lantern, or even to concentrate upon a lily in a vase on the altar or on a common bush in the churchyard. The selection however is justified on the ground that the object in question has certainly been employed (whether by the words of institution or by the common practice of Christians) as the vehicle for effecting a divine process of transformation in the spiritual nature and character of individual persons. Such an object must then be held to be eminently suitable for helping the individual to recall or recognise the wonder-working power of the divine presence. Moreover, as we have already observed, it is said that an omnipresent Spirit *is* where it acts or where we are *attending* to it.

In the above remarks I have tried to be as fair and as sympathetic as possible in my estimate of the position of those who earnestly desire my own Church to tolerate within its limits some kind of extra liturgical devotion, and I have tried to show the lines on which as it seems to me it is just possible for that toleration to proceed. Such a step would involve a new kind of comprehensiveness on the part of our Church. I must confess, however, that I am not myself so far convinced that that comprehensiveness should come about. Localised cultus of this sort lies completely outside the purview of the Founder of Christianity and of the line of prophets of which He is obviously the Crown. It involves a syncretism to which the whole atmosphere of Jewish theology was hostile. It certainly achieves quick results; but we may question whether it does not hinder many people from ever making real spiritual progress beyond a certain point, so that they never come to the full realisation of the presence in His full intensity of the invisible Christ beside them at every moment of their daily lives. Of course it may be held that such realisation is impossible save for a few spiritual aristocrats, and that we ought not to grudge less favoured souls their humbler means of access. I reject the latter conclusion however, because I do not see that we have any right to despair of the possibilities of the simple soul.

### SUMMARY

It is now our bounden duty to try to summarise the conclusions which have been arrived at from our survey. That we are concerned in the main with two entirely different modes of approach to the Divine

[ 85 ]

Presence (the symbolic and the direct) is I think an obvious conclusion, and I submit that it would be both unjust and unsympathetic to say that the method which proceeds by localisation is never valid and effective for those who make use of it. Let me therefore make a list of the various explanations of the facts which have been offered or may be offered, without indicating any personal preference.

(1) Localisation universally primitive.

(2) Localisation characteristic of the Aryan who gravitates between pantheism and an elaborate external cultus. The opposite form belongs to the Semitic temperament.

(3) Idolatry and iconoclasm due to preferences which cut across the barriers of race and which are temperamental, capable of developing irrespective of pedigree. It is pointed out that a single individual may in the course of a life-time swing over from the one type to the other. Each type is nevertheless held to correspond to a need. Both types are held to be equally valid.

(4) Localisation valid at a certain cultural level, but not when that level has been passed.

When reverted to by those who have previously discarded it, it has the nature of degeneracy.

(5) The transition from localisation to the worship with symbols, a sign of intellectual development. That which for want of a better term has been called Protestantism stresses scientific recognition rather than contemplative realisation. The view of Keyserling, who holds that localisation is as necessary for some experiences of the soul as its opposite.

(6) Localisation an accommodation to human weakness, drawing its origin from humble beginnings though much refined and civilised in its later development. Progress in religion demands that we should renounce its aid.

(7) The προσκύνησις of images legitimate but their λατρεία wrong. The former to be equated with the moderate use of alcohol and the moderate indulgence in gaming, and the latter with drunkenness and inordinate gambling. The Puritan will at once reject this, and it seems to me that it can hardly be an accident that the same temperament which rejects alcohol and gaming should also reject the προσκύνησις of material symbols as an avenue of approach to the Deity. Omitting alike any exaggerated re-

verence for the verbal injunctions to be found in the Scriptures and the associations of idolatry with obscene representations, it is evident that the Puritan (Heiler calls it the prophetic) temperament is led to adopt the attitude which it does, from some notion that the use of symbols in this manner is an invasion of the majesty and holiness of the Deity.

(8) Pure iconoclasm. All forms of localisation equally unsatisfactory. May be arrived at purely along philosophical lines, or by prophetic inspiration or tradition. In the former case will probably tolerate localisation for the uneducated but not in the latter. Holds the simplification effected to be so beneficial that no price is too great to pay for its introduction. Would in a few cases allow the reintroduction of emblems after a protracted period of education[1].

My readers may take their choice of these explanations.

I would conclude by referring to some extremely interesting reflections which oc-

---

[1] The difficulty of the pure iconoclast is that he sooner or later, on account of his own mental rhythms and finite consciousness, falls into some other kind of localisation.

## SUMMARY

cur in Professor Whitehead's recent book[1]
on the theory of symbols. He occupies
himself at one point with the variations in
attitude towards symbolism which have
characterised different epochs of civilisation, and contrasts the excessive symbolism
of the medieval period in Europe with the
reaction of the sixteenth century when
men tried to dispense with symbols as fond
things vainly invented, and concentrated on
their direct apprehension of the ultimate
facts. I venture to quote him a little, though
the whole of his book is important.

The attitude of mankind in this respect ex-
hibits (he says) an unstable mixture of attraction
and repulsion. The practical intelligence, the
theoretical desire to pierce to ultimate fact, and
ironic critical impulses have contributed the chief
motives towards the repulsion from symbolism.
Hard-headed men want facts and not symbols.
A clear theoretic intellect, with its generous
enthusiasm for the exact truth at all costs and
hazards, pushes aside symbols as being mere

[1] *Symbolism, its meaning and effect.* A. N. Whitehead,
Cambridge, 1928. (The Barbour-Page Lectures, U.S.A.)

# SUMMARY

make-believes, veiling and distorting that inner sanctuary of simple truth which reason claims as its own. The ironic critics of the follies of humanity have performed notable service in clearing away the lumber of useless ceremony symbolizing the degrading fancies of a savage past. The repulsion from symbolism stands out as a well-marked element in the cultural history of civilised people. There can be no reasonable doubt but that this continuous criticism has performed a necessary service in the promotion of a wholesome civilisation, both on the side of the practical efficiency of organised society, and on the side of a robust direction of thought.

No account of the uses of symbolism is complete without this recognition that the symbolic elements in life have a tendency to run wild, like the vegetation in a tropical forest. The life of humanity can easily be overwhelmed by its symbolic accessories. A continuous process of pruning, and of adaptation to a future ever requiring new forms of expression, is a necessary function in every society. The successful adaptation of old symbols to changes of social structure is the final mark of wisdom in sociological statesmanship. Also an occasional revolution in symbolism is required.

## SUMMARY

There is, however, a Latin proverb upon which, in our youth, some of us have been set to write themes. In English it reads thus: Nature, expelled with a pitchfork, ever returns. This proverb is exemplified by the history of symbolism. However you may endeavour to expel it, it ever returns. Symbolism is no mere idle fancy or corrupt degeneration: it is inherent in the very texture of human life. Language itself is a symbolism. And, as another example, however you reduce the functions of your government to their utmost simplicity, yet symbolism remains. It may be a healthier, manlier ceremonial, suggesting finer notions. But still it is symbolism. You abolish the etiquette of a royal court, with its suggestion of personal subordination, but at official receptions you ceremonially shake the hand of the Governor of your State. Just as the feudal doctrine of a subordination of classes, reaching up to the ultimate overlord, requires its symbolism; so does the doctrine of human equality obtain its symbolism. Mankind, it seems, has to find a symbol in order to express itself. Indeed "expression" is "symbolism."

When the public ceremonial of the State has been reduced to the barest simplicity, private clubs and associations at once commence to reconstitute symbolic actions. It seems as though mankind must always be masquerading. This imperative impulse suggests that the notion of an idle masquerade is the wrong way of thought about the symbolic elements in life. The function of these elements is to be definite, manageable, reproducible, and also to be charged with their own emotional efficacity: symbolic transference invests their correlative meanings with some or all of these attributes of the symbols, and thereby lifts the meanings into an intensity of definite effectiveness—as elements in knowledge, emotion, and purpose,—an effectiveness which the meanings may, or may not, deserve on their own account. The object of symbolism is the enhancement of the importance of what is symbolised.

It seems to me that anyone who is inclined to regard the practices of Catholicism and Hinduism with little sympathy must needs take account of this curious human drift or tendency to employ symbols charged with strong emotional significance for purposes of concentration and renewal especially in religion. As soon as these symbols are got rid of in one form they seem to

return in another. The simplificatory pro-
cesses of religious reformers often end in
the return of the jungle of natural religion.
If the abandonment of image cultus was a
real progressive simplification then it may
be that what we now see happening in
England is only an example of what happened in India with the gradual extinction
of Buddhism. There is a real principle in-
volved in resistance to this return of the
jungle, and I wish that my Catholic friends
would recognise it a little more. The proper
recognition of the relation of religion to art
is no valid excuse for the retention or reintroduction of an approach to the Deity
which might perhaps have been valid at a
lower and more primitive cultural level.

The fourteenth chapter of St Paul's
Epistle to the Romans may be regarded by
some of us as an able defence of the solution
of the problem with which we are faced
along the lines of toleration. The localiser
is not to judge or to be judged by him who
in his experience limits the Divine Presence

neither by space nor time. "To his own master he standeth or falleth." While however I throw this out as a tentative suggestion for a *modus vivendi* in the present distress, I would point out that the Apostle had no doubt in his own mind as to which of the two schools of thought referred to by him had the promise of the future in its grasp. The localiser like the Pharisaic Judaiser or the early apocalyptist may well belong to an order which is ready to vanish away.

(1) Perhaps I may be allowed to say in what sense I myself interpret the idea of a special localised presence. I accept the definition of the late Dr Rashdall, and I begin by recognising with the utmost reverence the all-pervading presence of God "having His centre everywhere and His circumference nowhere." I next recognise certain degrees of intensity in His activity in space-time, whereby we finite nuclei of consciousness have opportunities of experience which appear to us as localised. The choice of these occasions of intensity rests in the first instance with God Himself, but He allows us to extend the opportunities which they afford, and if we need them, to use emblems. Just as discovery and revelation are two aspects of the same intercommunion, so our attention to localised emblems and the action of God in mediating to us the grace of His personal influence through them are two aspects of the same thing. In the case of individuals such emblems need no special act of setting apart other than the deliberate choice by the individual; but there will be no guarantee that they will afford any help to other individuals. In the case of an emblem which is to have a

general or corporate significance and so to extend the opportunities of experience to a number of people it will obviously be convenient for a recognised leader of public and corporate devotion to set it apart and appoint it for the purpose in question. Beyond such a definition as this I do not feel that we are justified as Christians in proceeding. Those practices which depend upon the idea of a definitely restricted presence which, whatever we may say, is so closely tied to a material thing as in some way to interfere with its physical nature—such practices belong as has well been said to the religious twilight of mankind. They involve the adoption of a sacerdotal as distinct from a representative priesthood, and a theory of matter which we cannot to-day accept, and they are not in accordance with the religious simplification effected and employed by Jesus Christ, which had been prepared for by the Prophets, and was transmitted by the early Apostolic Ministry to our forefathers.

(2) I note that in the discussion which followed the reading of this paper Dr Oman of Westminster College summed up the problem about localisation in the form of two questions to which he said we ought carefully to think out the answer.

(*a*) What place should *form* take in the development of the religious plan?

(*b*) When is the material embodiment ceasing to be a help upward and becoming a step downward?

(3) *Concerning ὑπερδουλεία.*

When a certain famous Unitarian exclaimed: "I deny the Divinity of Christ? I do not deny the Divinity of any man": he was of course asserting his adherence to a fact of experience, i.e. that there is in each one of us a certain spark of Divinity: but he would be a rash individual who claimed that in each ordinary person there was an equal degree of the Divine Spirit localised, or that the presence of the Divine Spirit in the average man justified our giving to that average individual the same degree of worship which we feel justified in giving to the person of Christ. A distinction may of course with perfect propriety be drawn between the veneration given to persons and to things, to animate and to inanimate objects, since in the case of the former the fact that they are alive may seem to place them in a different category, and objects which are not alive can only, as I have tried to point out, be regarded as vehicles of the Divine Presence when they be-

come so as symbols charged with meaning, and
when by furnishing us with occasions and opportunities of experience they stimulate our emotions
and refresh our memories.

(4) I note the following interesting form of
localisation in the familiar hymn by the Roman
Catholic F. W. Faber:

> Jesu, gentlest Saviour,
> God of might and power,
> Thou Thyself art dwelling
> In us at this hour.
>
> Nature cannot hold Thee,
> Heaven is all too strait
> For Thine endless glory
> And Thy royal state.
>
> Out beyond the shining
> Of the furthest star
> Thou art ever stretching,
> Infinitely far.
>
> Yet the hearts of children
> Hold what worlds cannot
> And the God of wonders
> Loves the lowly spot.

The above, interpreted in conjunction with the
phrase "A Spirit is where it acts or where we are
attending to it," seems to me to satisfy all our
needs, and to give us all that we can desire in
reverent explanation of the glory and paradox of
the Christian experience.

For EU product safety concerns, contact us at Calle de José Abascal, 56–1°,
28003 Madrid, Spain or eugpsr@cambridge.org.

www.ingramcontent.com/pod-product-compliance
Ingram Content Group UK Ltd.
Pitfield, Milton Keynes, MK11 3LW, UK
UKHW020312140625
459647UK00018B/1839